MATH ON THE MOVE!

The Math of Motion

Written by Anne Rooney

WORLD BOOK

www.worldbook.com

Co-published by agreement between Shi Tu Hui and World Book, Inc.

Shi Tu Hui
Room 1807, Block 1,
#3 West Dawang Road
Chaoyang District, Beijing 100025
P.R. China

World Book, Inc.
180 North LaSalle Street
Suite 900
Chicago, Illinois 60601
USA

© 2026. All rights reserved. This volume may not be reproduced in whole or in part in any form without prior written permission from the publisher.

WORLD BOOK and the GLOBE DEVICE are registered trademarks or trademarks of World Book, Inc.

Library of Congress Control Number: 2025942230

Aha! Academy: Math
ISBN: 978-0-7166-7377-4 (set, hardcover)

Math on the Move! The Math of Motion
ISBN: 978-0-7166-7387-3 (hard cover)
ISBN: 978-0-7166-7450-4 (e-book)
ISBN: 978-0-7166-7440-5 (soft cover)

Staff

Editorial

Vice President
Tom Evans

Editorial Project Coordinator
Kaile Kilner

Senior Curriculum Designer
Caroline Davidson

Curriculum Designer
Mikayla Kightlinger

Proofreader
Nathalie Strassheim

Indexer
Nathaniel Lindstrom

Graphics and Design

Senior Visual
Communications Designer
Melanie Bender

Designer
Shannon Hagman

Written by Anne Rooney

Designed by Starletta Polster

Acknowledgments

The publishers gratefully acknowledge the following sources for photography. All illustrations were prepared by WORLD BOOK unless otherwise noted.

Cover: Elenamiv/Shutterstock; Jenny Sturm/Shutterstock; Joel Rice/Shutterstock; pio3/Shutterstock; Wirestock Creators/Shutterstock

NASA/Aero Animation/Ben Schweighart 19; © Space Frontiers/Stringer/Archive Photos/Getty Images 39; NASA 5, 9, 31, 32, 33; © Shutterstock 4, 5, 6, 7, 8, 9, 10, 11, 12, 13, 14, 15, 16, 17, 18, 19, 20, 21, 22, 23, 24, 25, 26, 27, 28, 29, 30, 31, 33, 34, 35, 36, 37, 38, 39, 40, 41, 42, 43, 44, 45, 46, 47, 48

There is a glossary of terms on page 48. Terms defined in the glossary are in type that looks like *this* on their first appearance on any spread (two facing pages).

Contents

Introduction 4

① **On the move** **6**
    Get moving! 8
    Straight on, left, right... 10
    North, south, east, west 12

② **Going and stopping** **14**
    Speed demons 16
    Faster and faster—but going nowhere 18
    Blast off! 20
    Collision! 22
    Dead stop 24

③ **Around and around** **26**
    Escape from the center 28
    Gravity and orbits 30
    Fly to Mars! 32

④ **Motion and shape** **34**
    Streamlining—submarines, jets, etc 36
    Gently down 38
    Trajectories 40
    Totally random! 42

Program a person! 44
Index 46
Glossary 48

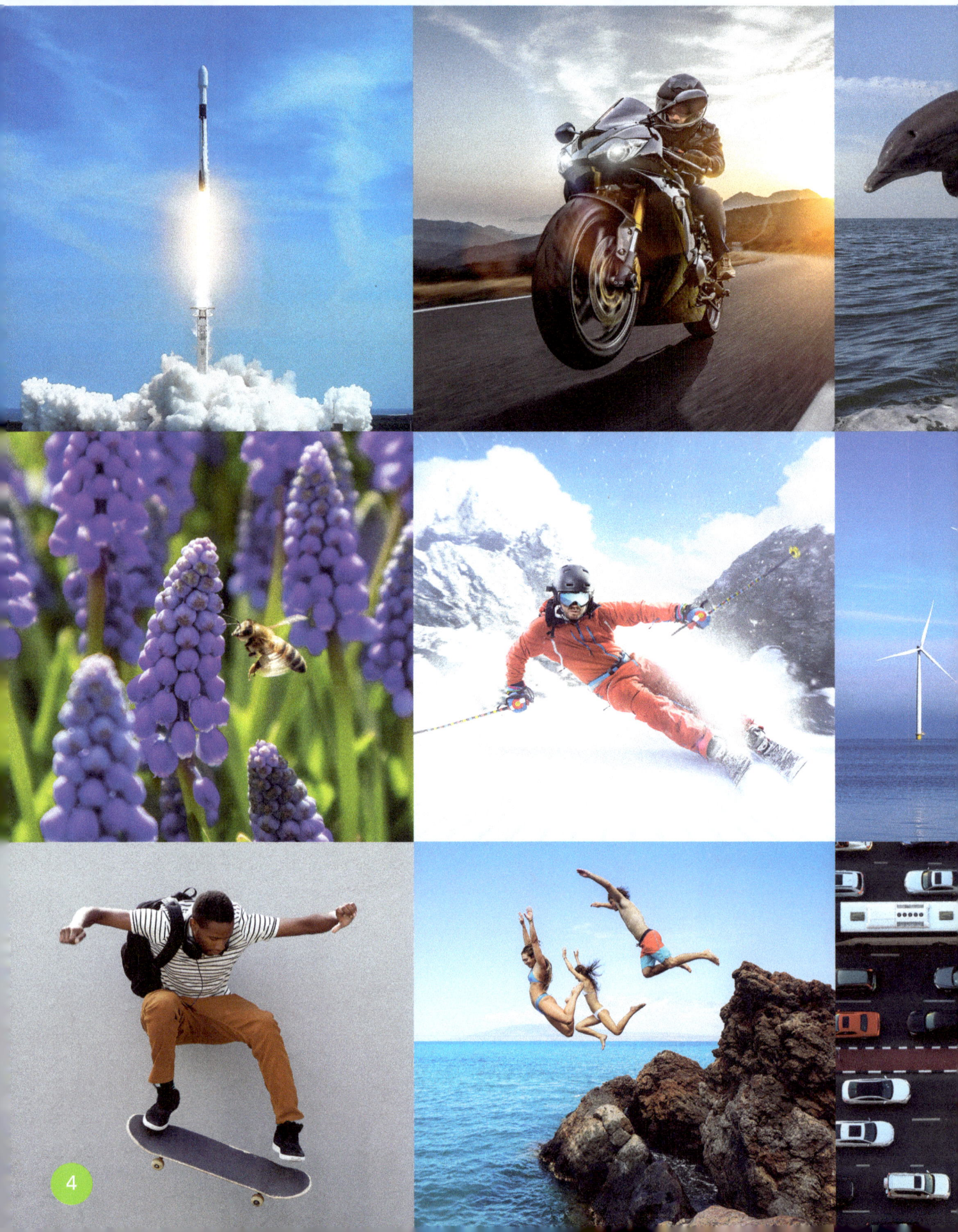

Introduction

You're moving all the time, even when you don't realize it. Everything around you moves, too—and we're all on a planet whizzing through space. Movement is everywhere!

Things move because of forces acting on them. We can explore these forces with math. And we can use math to describe how things move—the directions they go in, their speed, how far they move, and what happens when they meet something else, either moving or still.

Let's see how math can help us understand the ever-moving world around us.

ON THE MOVE

1

We can use math to work out exactly how things move, when they will move or stop, and how fast and how far they will go. The math of movement is the same for everything, whether it's a living thing, a machine, or just something carried by the wind or water.

I can move faster than you!

Look around you: you can probably see some things that are moving and some that are still. Whether things move or stay still is the result of forces.

Things can move from one place to another, but they can also move and end up back where they started! You move up and down when you jump on a trampoline. A turning wind turbine moves round and round. The piston in an engine moves in and out. We can describe all these movements with math.

Pistons move up and down.

I'm getting dizzy!

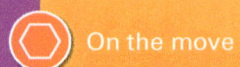
On the move

Get moving!

Nothing will move unless a *force* acts to start it off. For an object, that might be a push or a pull. For a living thing that decides to move, the force comes from its muscles.

To move, something must go in a direction. If it moves backward and forward, up and down, or round and round, it changes direction frequently— but it always has a direction.

Math explains how things move using direction, speed, and distance.

Forward!

Think of something that's not moving, such as a book on a table. What will make it start moving? It would move if you picked it up, nudged it across the table, pushed it off the edge, or tilted the table. But it won't just start moving on its own.

When you float, you don't move unless you push yourself along—or someone else pushes you!

The skateboarder pushes off with her foot (muscle power) to move forward, and *gravity* pulls her board downward.

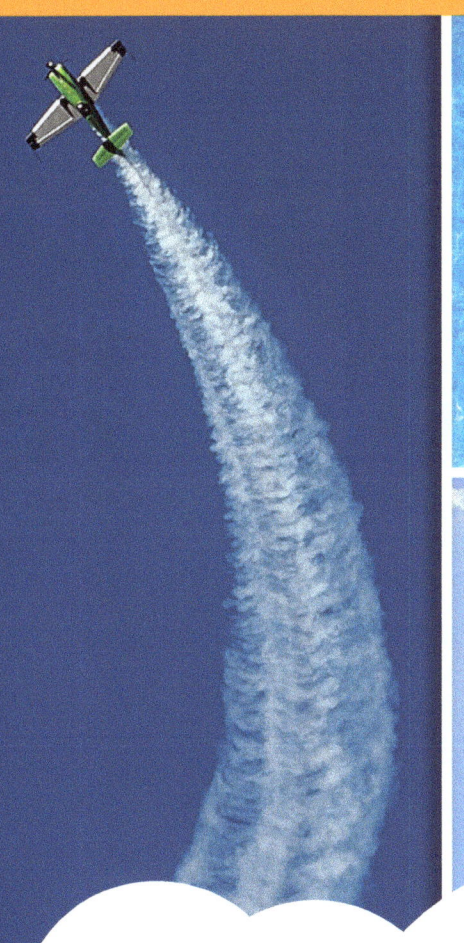

Katherine Johnson worked at NASA as a mathematician. As a Black woman in a racially segregated United States, she broke many barriers with her work. She calculated the paths for the first American crewed spacecraft in 1961 and for the moon landing of 1969. She had to figure out the speed and direction the Apollo craft needed to meet up with the moving moon at the right time.

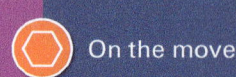
On the move

Straight on, left, right…

When you know the starting point for moving, you can use directions like "left," "right," "forward," "up," and "down." If you are outside the front door of your home and someone says "go left 50 yards," that's clear. But if you came out of a different door, left might be in the opposite direction. We need to be careful. These directions are *relative* to the starting point, because they are specific to where you start from.

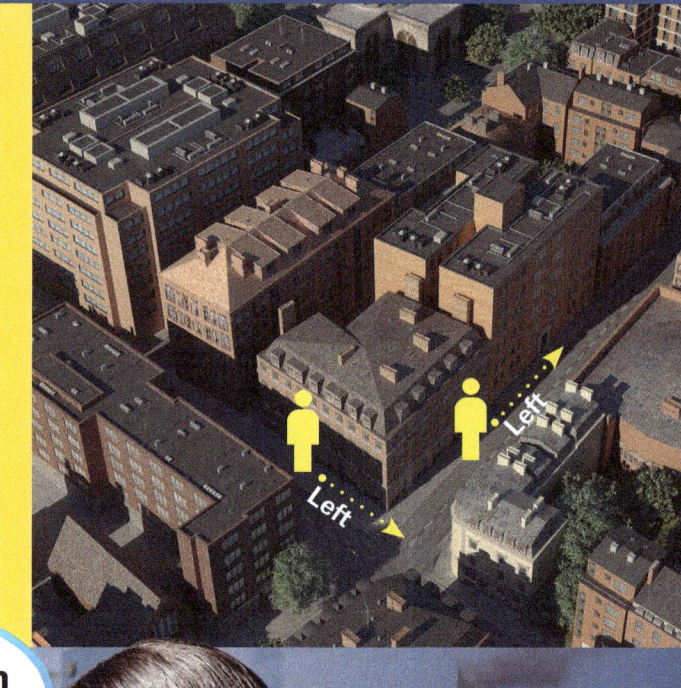

Then turn right…

TECH TIME

GPS is the system used by mapping apps and in-car *satellite* navigation systems to give directions. It bounces radio waves off satellites above Earth and calculates exact positions from the time it takes for signals to return. Then it uses math to find the best route between where you are and where you want to go.

Moving between two points involves a direction and a distance. This is true whether it's a walk between your kitchen and bedroom, or a space flight between Earth and Neptune!

The shortest distance between two points on a flat surface is a straight line. It's always shorter than a wiggly or crooked path. But we can't always go in a straight line. There might be obstacles in the way, or you might have to follow existing paths. Your route will be described by direction and distances, such as "go left 50 yards, then turn right and go 100 yards."

The longest side (hypotenuse) of a right triangle is always shorter than the other two sides added together

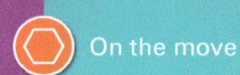
On the move

North, south, east, west

We can describe turns using angles. A full turn (a circle) has 360 degrees. If you keep going forward, you are not turning, so that's 0 degrees. If you turned around to go back the way you came, that would be a 180-degree turn.

There's no path here!

If you're going south and you turn 90 degrees clockwise, you go west. If you turn 45 degrees, you go south-west. This angle is measured *relative* to the direction you are currently facing and is called a relative bearing. Where a turn of 20 degrees will take you depends on where you are heading to start with.

Walking along the street, you can only turn at a corner or junction, but not everywhere has fixed paths! In a boat or plane, or walking over a field, you can turn anywhere in any direction. Then angles and directions like north and south are useful.

The U.S. Army gives directions in the form N35E, which means "head 35 degrees eastward from the north," or S17W, which means "head 17 degrees westward from the south." These are *absolute* bearings. With a distance and a *bearing*, we can pinpoint any location.

CURIOUS CONNECTIONS

BIOLOGY Honey bees use a waggle dance to communicate direction and distance. A bee that has found food dances to show the angle and distance to it. With just this information, other bees can reach the food.

Food 200 feet that way!

2
GOING AND STOPPING

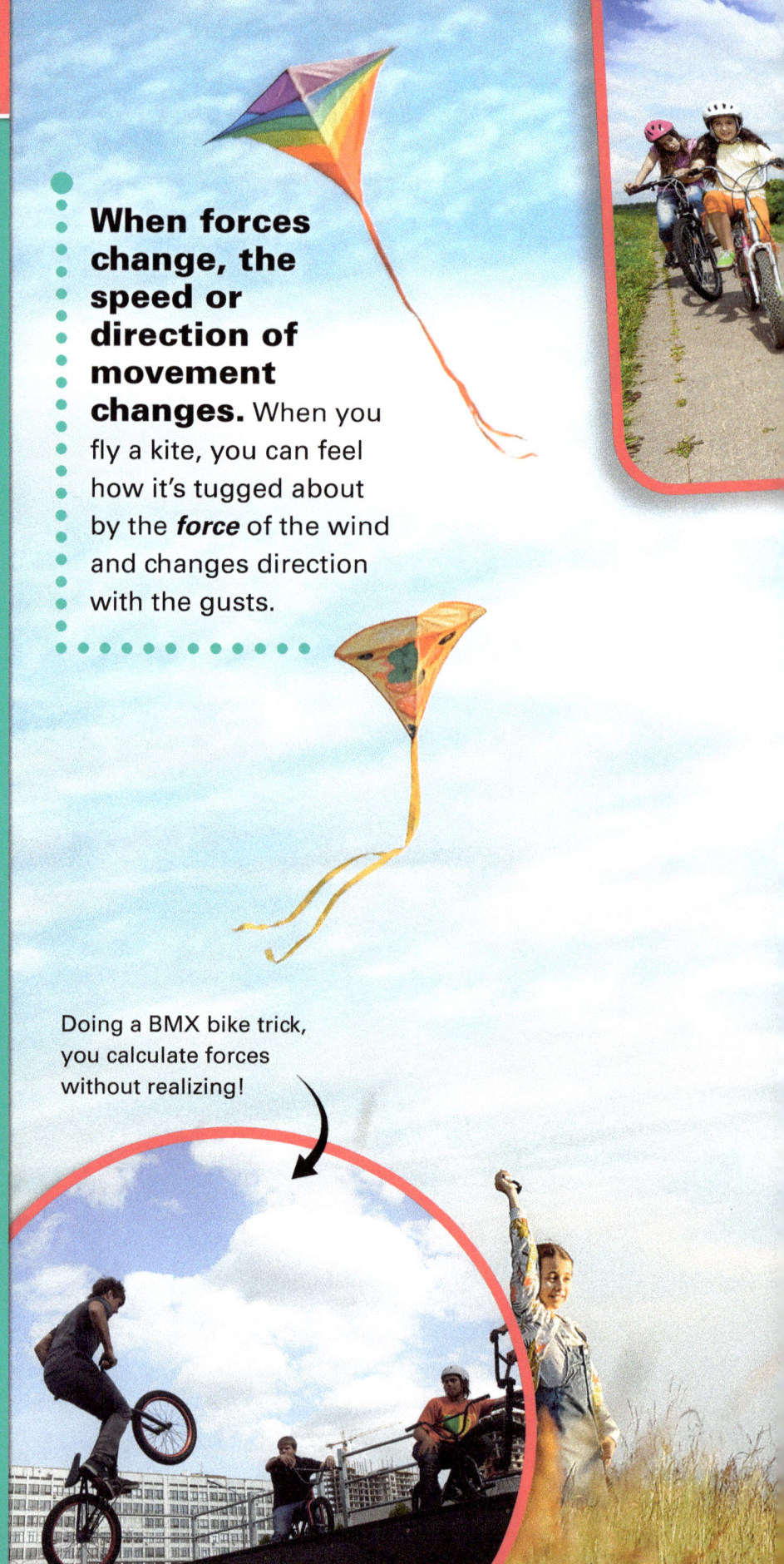

When forces change, the speed or direction of movement changes. When you fly a kite, you can feel how it's tugged about by the *force* of the wind and changes direction with the gusts.

Doing a BMX bike trick, you calculate forces without realizing!

Forces control when and how things move. We can use math to calculate how far something will move, which direction it will go in, how fast it will go—and what happens to its energy when it stops!

We calculate forces automatically while riding a bike, walking, or using rollerblades. If you want to cycle faster, you push the pedals of your bike round faster, using more force. If you want to turn, you lean your bike and body, or turn the handlebars, using a turning force.

Let's take a look at the math behind going faster, going slower, stopping—and even colliding.

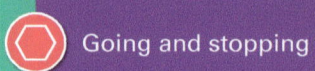
Going and stopping

Speed demons

We often measure speed in miles per hour (mph), but it can also be in feet per second or other units. To calculate speed, we divide the distance something moves by the time it takes.

If you walked six miles in two hours, you would be going at
6 ÷ 2 = 3 miles each hour, or 3 mph.

Some typical speeds

560 mph

30 mph

0.03 mph—
about 32 inches per minute!

How fast can you run? The faster you run, the higher your speed. Speed is measured as how far something travels in a fixed period of time.

You can work out how far something will move in a given time if you know its speed.

A car going at 30 mph for three hours will travel 30 x 3 = 90 miles.

And if you know how far something has to travel and its speed, you can work out how long it will take to get there.

A plane flying 2,000 miles at 500 mph will take 2,000 ÷ 500 = 4 hours to complete its flight.

CURIOUS CONNECTIONS

ASTRONOMY

Did you know the universe has a speed limit? Nothing can go faster than the speed of light! Light travels through space at about 186,000 miles per second, or 671 million mph. It takes light about 8 minutes to reach Earth from the sun.

SPEED LIMIT 671,000,000

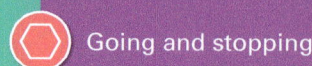
Going and stopping

Faster and faster— but going nowhere

Speed tells us how far something moves in a specific time. It can be along a wiggly or straight path. But *velocity* measures *displacement*—how far from its original position something moves—in a set time.

On a winding road, a car might have a high speed but a low velocity.

If you ran along the two short sides of this triangle in a minute, your speed would be 30 + 40 = 70 feet per minute. But your velocity would be only 50 feet per minute, as you end up 50 feet away from your starting point. If you run in a circle, your velocity is zero because you end back where you started!

30 ft

70 ft

40 ft

On a carousel, you might start slowly and go faster and faster—you accelerate! But your velocity is zero—how does that work?

It's a fast ride—with zero velocity!

Acceleration is a change in speed. It's a measure of how much the speed changes. If a cheetah increases its speed by 7 mph with each stride, it's going at 7 mph after the first stride, 14 mph after two strides, 21 mph after three strides, and so on.

We calculate acceleration as

$$\frac{\text{final speed} - \text{starting speed}}{\text{time}}$$

So, a cheetah going from 0 to 30 mph in 5 seconds accelerates at

$$\frac{30 - 0 \text{ mph}}{5 \text{ seconds}}$$

$$= 6 \text{ mph per second}$$

TECH TIME

Someday spacecraft might use solar sails. This technology is designed to use the momentum of solar wind, the constant stream of photons (particles of light) given off by the sun. When a photon strikes a solar sail, the surface reflects the photon back into space. Some of the photon's momentum (amount of motion) is transferred to the sail. When the solar sail reflects the photons back into space, the photons exert a force on the sail.

Going and stopping

Blast off!

When a rocket launches into space, the *force* of the gases blasting out of the back is the same as the force pushing the rocket upward. Space engineers figure out how much fuel to burn to get the force needed to raise the rocket. We use the same trick without doing the math all the time in our daily life!

If you go swimming, you pull water back with your arms to force your body forward through the water. The more force you use, the faster and farther you travel through the water.

A tennis player might hit the ball with a force of 200 *newtons*. This pushes the ball forward through the air. But the ball pushes back against the racket at the same time. The force travels up the handle to the player's shoulder, which is why injuries happen!

How far and fast the ball goes depends on the force the tennis player uses to hit it.

Isaac Newton noticed that every action produces an equal reaction in the opposite direction. We see this all the time in motion. Calculating the *force* of the action tells us the force of the reaction.

Doing a skateboard trick, the rider learns how much speed they need to launch the board with enough force to keep it aloft for the trick—and how hard they need to push off to get that speed.

An octopus sucks in water and forces it out of its siphon, pushing the octopus forward with the same force that the water has going backward.

CAREER CORNER

A rocket burns fuel to leave the ground, but carrying fuel makes the rocket heavier, so then it needs even more fuel! **Ballistics** engineers use math to figure out the right balance of fuel and weight for a rocket.

Going and stopping

Collision!

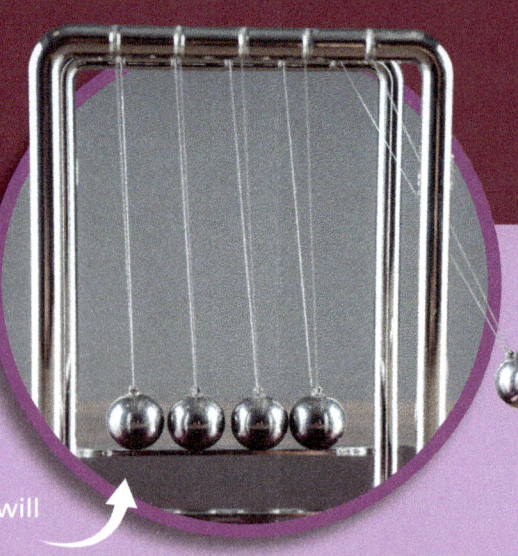

Energy can't be created or destroyed, it can only be transferred or change type. The energy going into a crash must be the same as the energy coming out of a crash.

When the swinging ball strikes the others, the energy moves through them and the ball on the left will swing outwards.

total energy before collision = total energy after collision

A collision often makes something else move. If you roll a ball to hit a bowling pin, the energy from the ball transfers to the bowling pin and knocks it over.

DID YOU KNOW?

The biggest crash in Earth's history happened more than four billion years ago. A planet-sized object smashed into Earth, and the heat *vaporized* part of Earth and the colliding object. The leftovers formed into the moon!

Crash! When objects collide, the movement energy has to go somewhere!

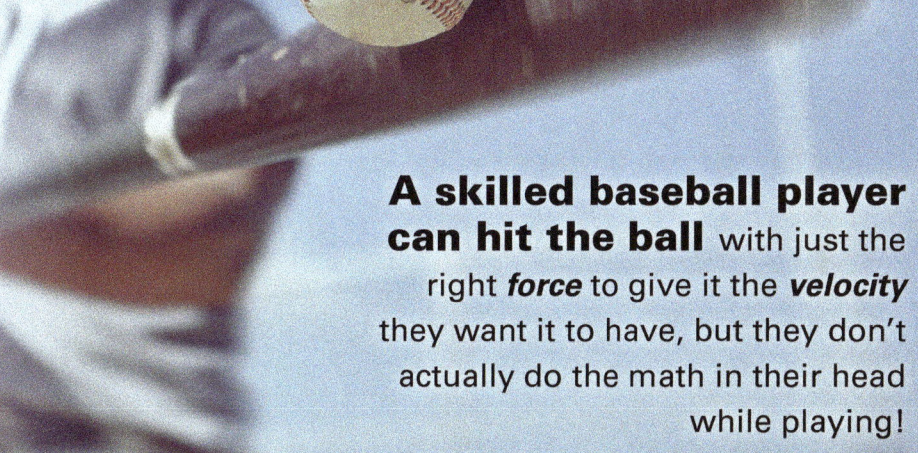

When you hit a baseball, the bat and ball are moving in opposite directions. Energy from the ball pushes against the bat, slowing it. But you're swinging the bat with more energy. It transfers its energy to the ball, which flies off. Using math, we can work out the speed of the ball and the direction it will go in.

A skilled baseball player can hit the ball with just the right *force* to give it the *velocity* they want it to have, but they don't actually do the math in their head while playing!

Pool players do more calculations. They figure out the angle to strike a ball to make it go where they want, and send the balls that it collides with to good positions. There's a lot of math in this: the speed, force, and angle of contact come together to make a winning or losing shot!

Going and stopping

Dead stop

When a car crashes into a tree, the tree doesn't start moving!
The car's movement energy is changed to other types of energy. The metal of the car is bent, there is a loud noise, and a lot of energy escapes as heat. Calculating the energy and controlling how it is released is vital to making cars safer when they crash.

What happens when something stops moving in a collision—where does the energy go? Energy can't just disappear. Mathematicians can work out from the *velocity*, angle, and mass of colliding objects what will happen.

The surface of the moon is covered in craters made by asteroids (rocks from space) crashing into the surface. The energy of the fast-moving rock goes into smashing a hole in the surface and into heat. Experts can work out the size of an asteroid from measuring the crater that it made.

CAREER CORNER

Crash engineers are experts at figuring out the math of car crashes. They model crashes on computers and create real collisions using crash-test dummies in cars. The information is used to design cars so that they absorb the energy of a crash in a safe way.

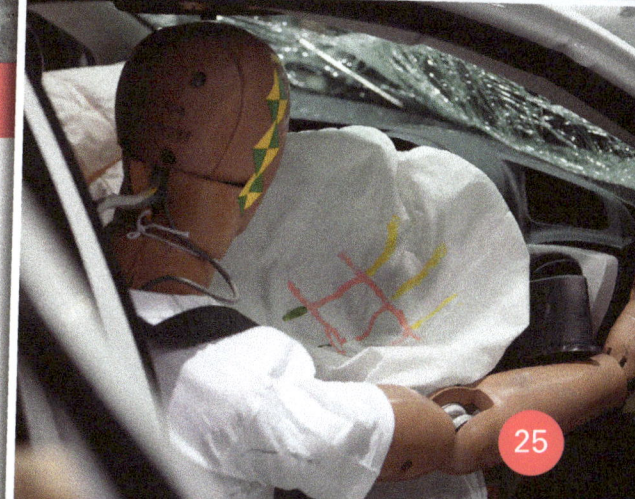

3
AROUND AND AROUND

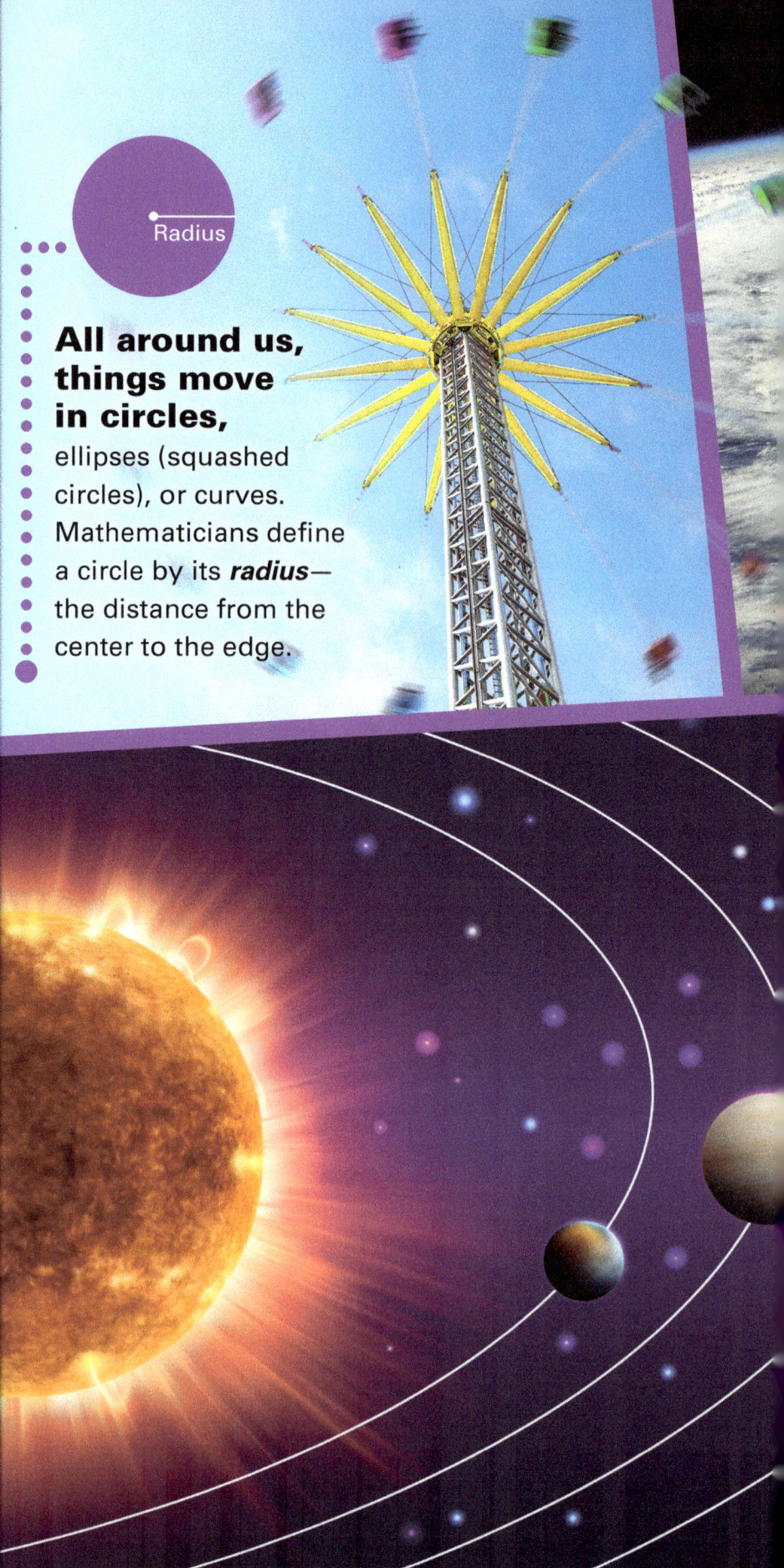

All around us, things move in circles, ellipses (squashed circles), or curves. Mathematicians define a circle by its *radius*—the distance from the center to the edge.

Some things move only in circles. The math of these is finely balanced: if one *force* grows larger or smaller, the object will go off in a straight line or fall to the middle of the circle.

Understanding the math of circular motion helps in many fields, from planning flight paths for planes to setting speed limits on winding roads. It's really important in astronomy and space travel because almost everything in space moves in a circle or ellipse.

In 1604, German mathematician and astronomer **Johannes Kepler** worked out that the paths of the planets around the sun are ellipses, not circles. He worked this out by studying how Mars appears to move in the night sky, recognizing that both Mars and Earth are moving—a tricky set of calculations!

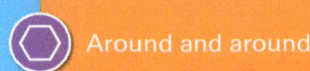 Around and around

Escape from the center

The *force* that prevents something moving in a circle from escaping is called a ***centripetal force*. *Gravity*** is the centripetal force that keeps the moon going around Earth. In a salad spinner, the walls of the basket provide the centripetal force, stopping the lettuce escaping.

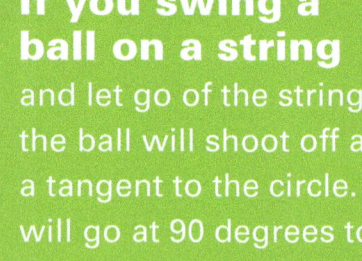

I can't get away!

Momentum* makes an object** want to keep moving in the same direction. When it's spinning, the same direction changes all the time. At any point, the object would escape along a straight line at a right angle to the ***radius of the circle. Mathematicians call this line a ***tangent*** to the circle.

If you swing a ball on a string and let go of the string, the ball will shoot off at a tangent to the circle. It will go at 90 degrees to the string, which forms the radius of the circle.

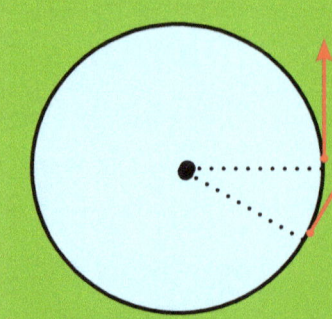

If you've ever used a salad spinner or been on a roundabout, you'll already know that things moving quickly in a circle are thrown outwards. If they keep going around, it's because they can't escape!

Clouds escape the edge of a hurricane at a tangent to the spiral.

In a salad spinner or spin dryer, water is thrown toward the side of the spinning drum and goes through holes to fall away.

CURIOUS CONNECTIONS

ART Spin art paintings are made by dropping paint onto a spinning canvas. As the paint is thrown outward, away from the center of the turning canvas, it makes dramatic radiating patterns.

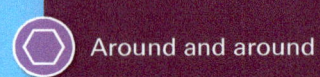 Around and around

Gravity and orbits

Isaac Newton showed that the effect of *gravity* decreases as the distance between two objects increases. The inverse square law works here. When the distance doubles, the ***force*** of gravity drops to a quarter, because $2^2 = 4$ and the inverse of 4 is ¼. If the distance trebles, gravity reduces to one ninth, because $3^2 = 9$.

Inverse Square Law

 Gravity = 1

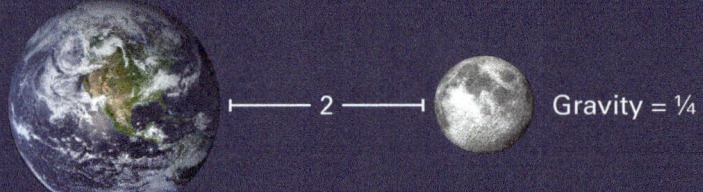 Gravity = ¼

A *satellite* is kept aloft by balanced forces. Before launching a satellite, scientists figure out how far up and how fast it must go so that its speed and the pull of gravity balance to keep it up. If it went too fast, it would hurtle off into space. If it went too slowly, it would fall back to Earth.

In space there are lots of circles! Planets go around stars, and stars *orbit* the center of a galaxy. It takes a lot of math to figure out how moons, planets, and spacecraft will move as gravity acts on them.

The Clipper craft going to Jupiter's moon Europa used the gravity of Mars to accelerate it in the right direction.

In 1925, before there were any spacecraft, mathematician **Friedrich Zander** figured out how to change the *velocity* of spacecraft using the gravity of moons or planets they passed. As a craft comes near a planet, gravity pulls it in. Using the right path, the craft can speed up but go past, changing direction. This is now called a "gravity assist" maneuver.

Gravity Assist Maneuver

Spacecraft accelerates

Fly to Mars!

Around and around

Mars and Earth move around the sun at different speeds, and the distance between them changes constantly. In 2003, Mars and Earth were just 34.8 million miles (56 million kilometers) apart, but that won't happen again until 2237.

Scientists planning a trip between the two planets need to figure out the best launch time to make the trip as short as possible—but without having to wait too long. Mars and Earth line up quite closely every 26 months, offering a good launch window.

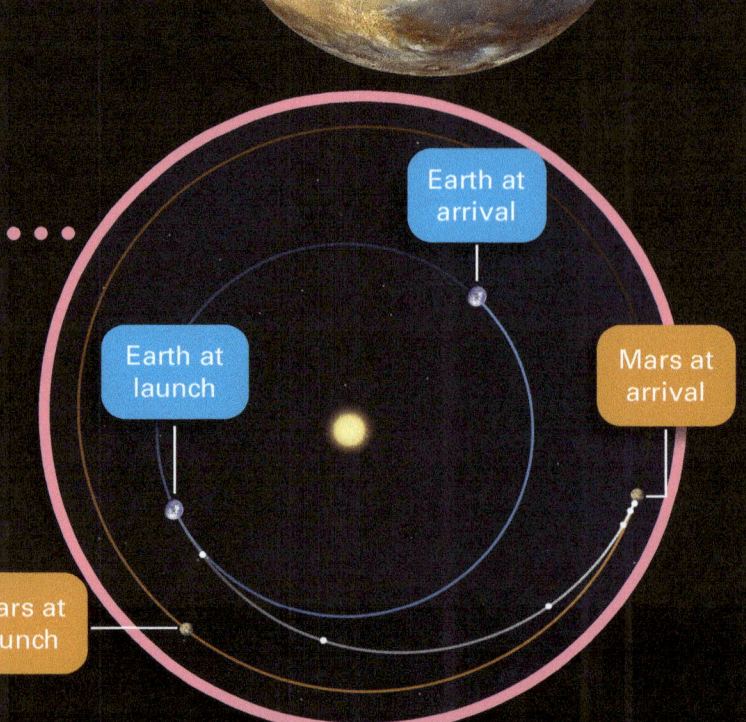

Sending a spacecraft to another planet takes a lot of complex math. It's not like going from one place to another on Earth because both the starting point and the destination are moving all the time!

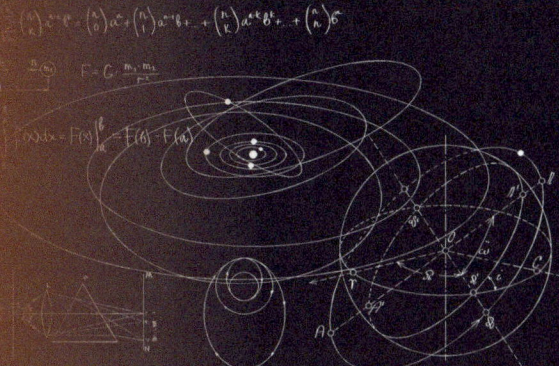

A spacecraft must approach at the right angle, in the right place, and at the right time to reach the chosen landing site. The planet is rotating as well as moving through space, so it's a tricky set of sums!

Gravity **pulls an approaching spacecraft downward.** A parachute and small rockets blasting downward work against gravity to slow it down so it doesn't crash into the surface.

TECH TIME

The rover Perseverance carried the tiny helicopter Ingenuity to Mars to take photos and hunt out interesting locations. A lot of math was needed to work out how to make Ingenuity fly in the very thin atmosphere of Mars.

4 MOTION AND SHAPE

All substances are made of tiny particles— atoms and *molecules*—and slow the movement of something moving through them. The shape of something affects how easily and quickly it moves.

Friction **happens when one substance rubs against another,** making *resistance* to movement. If you push something over the floor, friction makes it hard to push. There is friction between a surface and water or air, too. We usually call it *drag*.

Spacecraft move through the *vacuum* of space, but everything on Earth moves through some substance, such as air, water, or even soil or rock.

In space, there is no friction, so shape doesn't affect movement.

34

Math helps engineers design shapes that can move smoothly and quickly by studying the flow of water or air over a surface.

What we want something to do affects how it's designed. We want a train or plane to move quickly and efficiently, saving fuel. But we want a parachute to help something come slowly down to Earth. Engineers design shapes to move quickly, or slowly, as needed.

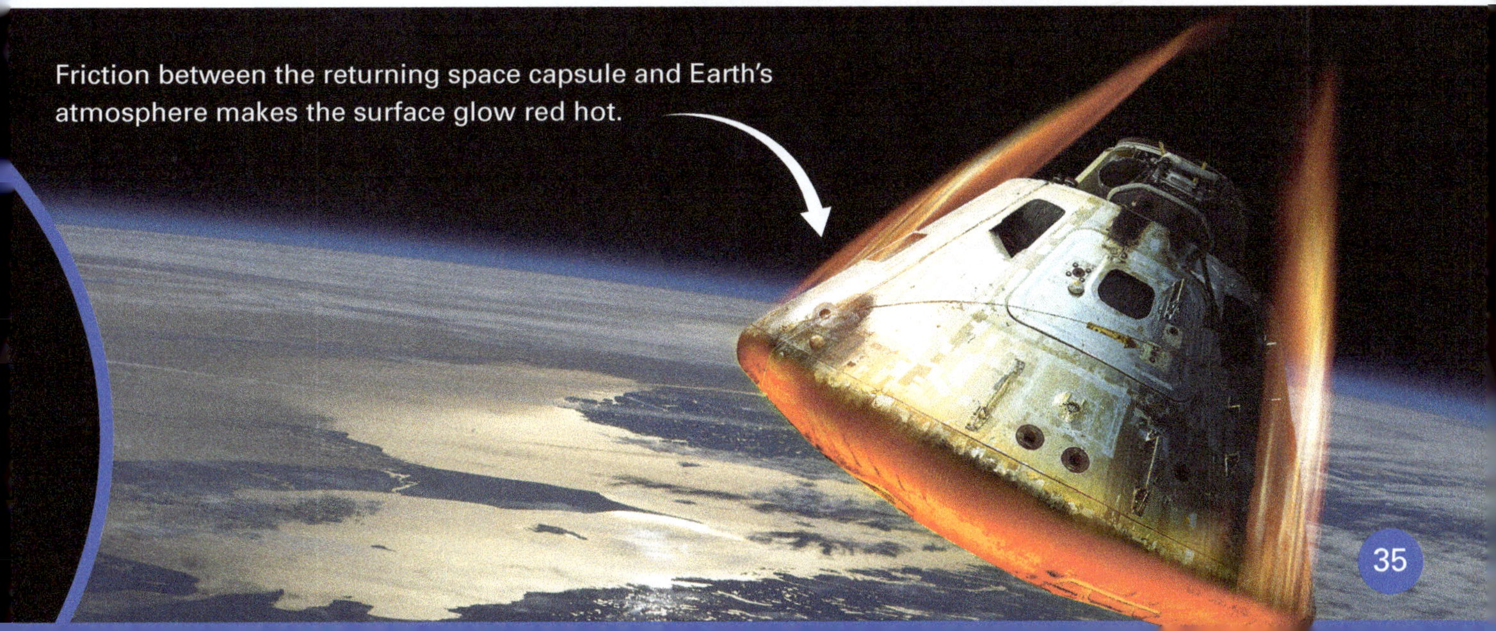

Friction between the returning space capsule and Earth's atmosphere makes the surface glow red hot.

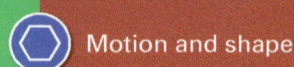

Motion and shape

Streamlining—submarines, jets, etc.

Being *streamlined* is all about shape. Engineers copy shapes from nature to make vehicles streamlined. If you compare the front of an earthworm and the front of a bullet train, you'll see they are the same shape!

As water or air passes over the surface of a moving object, it creates *drag*, slowing the movement. If the surface area is small, there will be less drag. A shape with a simple outline and a smooth surface is best.

I'm one of the most streamlined animals there is!

Burrowing animals often have a tube-shaped body and a pointed nose.

36

A streamlined shape slips easily through air or water.

It has smooth, flat sides, and is usually narrow at the front, and longer than it is wide. Animals that move quickly through water have naturally *evolved* a streamlined shape, from seals and birds to fish.

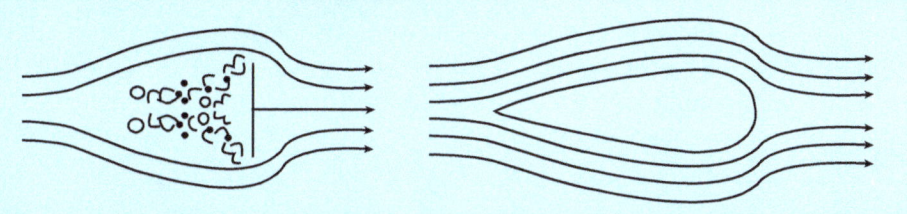

Smooth, curved lines move more easily than abrupt angles.
Imagine pushing a rectangular box and a football through water. The football will glide more easily. Water falling around the angles of the box will create eddies and currents.

Even a slow container ship is pointed at the front end to cut through the water.

Engineers test vehicle designs in a wind tunnel to check they are streamlined.

DID YOU KNOW?

People race super-fast, streamlined vehicles over the Salt Flats of Bonneville, Utah, and the Black Rock Desert of Nevada. The record for fastest vehicle on land was set in 1997 by Anthony Green driving ThrustSSC at 763 mph—the first land vehicle to break the sound barrier!

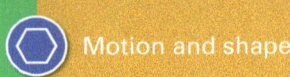

Motion and shape

Gently down

Sycamore seeds

Many seeds have a shape that helps them to be carried gently by the wind rather than falling straight down. Sycamore seeds whirl around as their two wings are blown by the wind. The seed of a dandelion works rather like a parachute. Air trapped under a wide shape holds an object up. *Gravity* pulling it down squashes the air underneath, creating pressure that holds the object up, whether it's a seed or a parachute.

Spreading its wings to trap air slows a diving eagle so it doesn't crash into the ground!

A *streamlined* shape makes quick movement easy, but sometimes we want to slow things down instead!

Math lets us figure out how quickly something will fall.

Objects falling on Earth accelerate at about 32 feet per second per second (32 ft/s^2), ignoring *air resistance*. That means that after one second, it's moving at 32 ft/s, after two seconds it's moving at 64 ft/s, and so on. On Earth, air usually gets in the way and slows things down. You can test this yourself by dropping a flat sheet of paper and a sheet you've crumpled up at the same time.

Italian scientist Galileo Galilei figured out that objects of the same shape but different masses fall at the same rate. Shape changes the rate of fall because of air resistance. He was proved right in 1971 when astronaut **David Scott** dropped a hammer and a feather on the moon and both hit the ground at the same time!

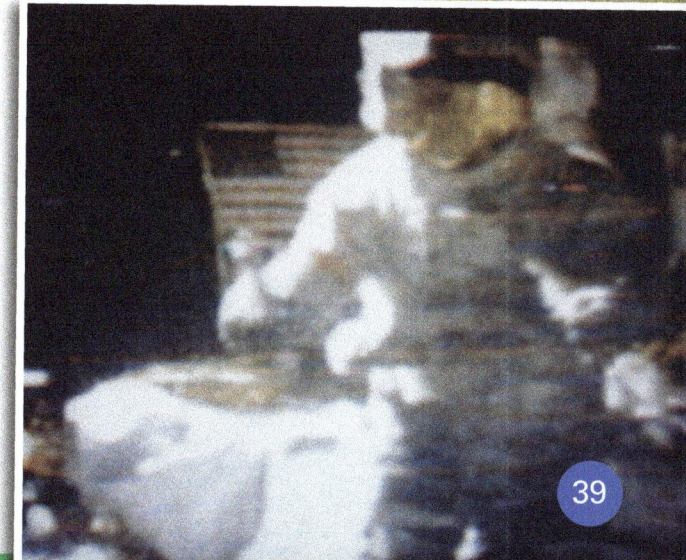

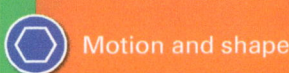

Motion and shape

Trajectories

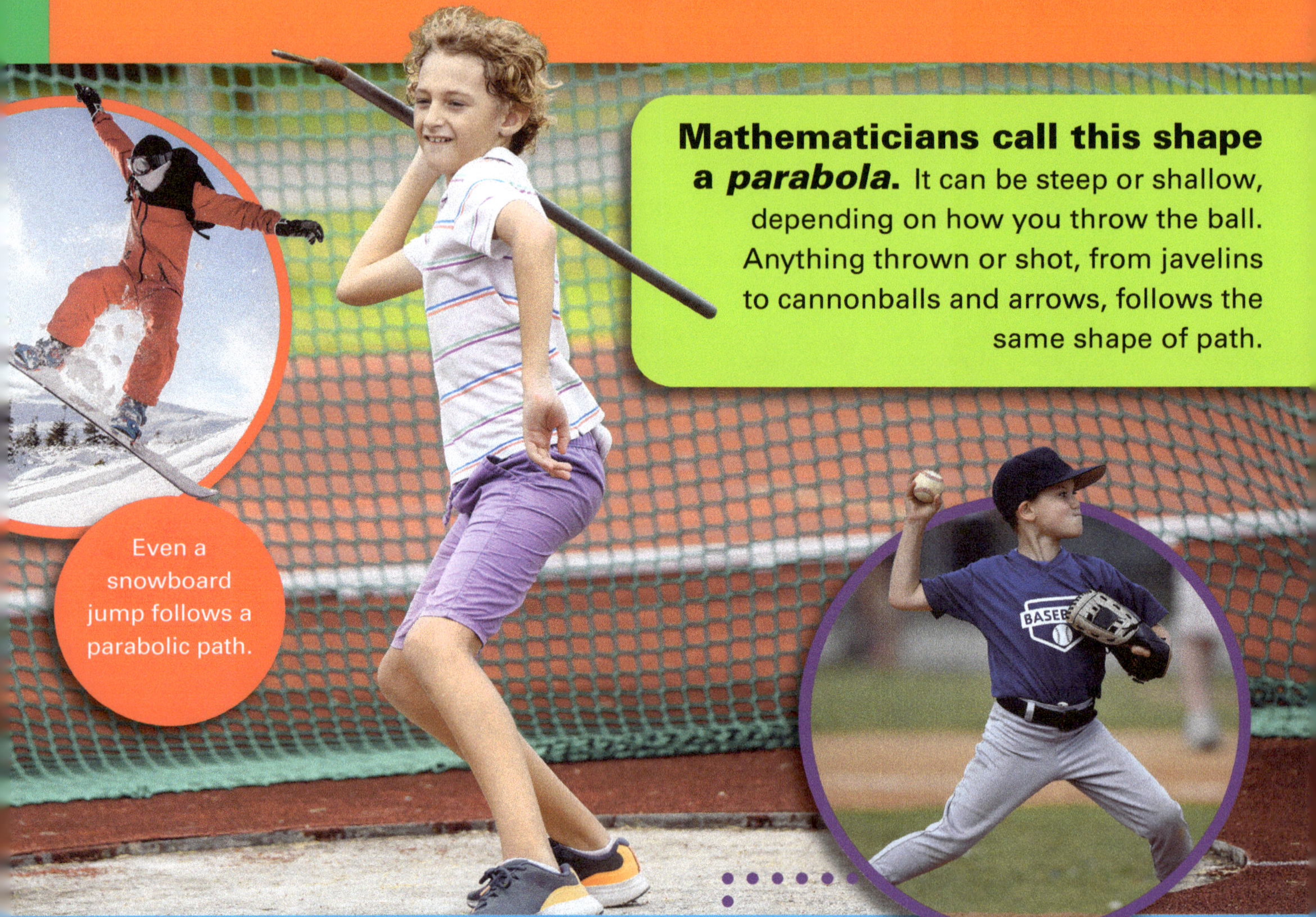

Mathematicians call this shape a *parabola*. It can be steep or shallow, depending on how you throw the ball. Anything thrown or shot, from javelins to cannonballs and arrows, follows the same shape of path.

Even a snowboard jump follows a parabolic path.

The *force* you use to throw a ball works against *gravity*. After a short time, though, gravity begins to drag it downward. It can still move forward because it has *momentum*, but it's going downward at the same time—until it hits the ground.

Sports players need to understand how the angle of their throw affects the *trajectory* of the ball they hit or throw. Without realizing it, they do a lot of math to work out their pitch!

40

Have you ever noticed the path of a ball when you throw it? The path, called a trajectory, is usually curved as the ball goes up, loops over the high point, and falls down again.

How far a ball will go depends on how much force you use to throw it and the angle at which you throw it. The steeper the angle, the higher the ball will go, but it won't travel as far along. But if you throw at a very shallow angle, it can hit the ground before it's used up all its energy because gravity wins out too soon. Then it will bounce!

Yesssss!

DID YOU KNOW?

Astronaut Alan Shepard hit a golf ball on the moon in 1971. The ball still followed a parabolic path. The moon has lower gravity than Earth, which would help the ball go farther before falling to the ground. But the lack of air means there is no lift, and this reduces the distance the ball can travel. Shepard's best shot went only 40 yards (36.5 meters)!

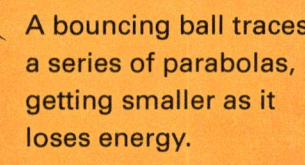
A bouncing ball traces a series of parabolas, getting smaller as it loses energy.

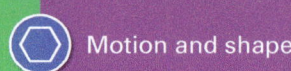 Motion and shape

Totally random!

Pressure is the push against a surface. The more the particles are moving, the higher the pressure. Blowing up a balloon forces lots of air into a small space. Air particles moving randomly inside bump into the skin of the balloon, inflating the balloon.

At the tiniest scale, lots of motion is random— but that doesn't mean it's not important. The smallest particles move around randomly, but they create the pressures and currents that move larger objects. We do a lot of math from these random movements!

Pollen on the surface of water is bumped around by the moving water *molecules*.

When the wind blows, lots of molecules in the air move in the same direction. The pressure of the wind moves objects it strikes, such as a flag or wind turbine. We can measure the wind's pressure in units, such as pounds per square inch, or its speed in miles per hour. Scientists can figure out how much electricity they will get from a wind turbine at different wind speeds, putting math to work to manage the flow of electricity. We don't need to know the movements of individual particles to predict larger movements.

CURIOUS CONNECTIONS

ASTRONOMY The photons (parcels of energy) created in the heart of the sun move randomly, bouncing off other particles until they finally stream out as sunlight. Their path twists and turns and reverses so much it can take millions of years for a *photon* to escape—and then it reaches Earth in just eight minutes!

43

Program a person!

You will need:
- String or chalk
- A surface with large square or rectangular tiles or paving slabs
- A friend
- A stopwatch (it can be on a phone)
- A measuring tape
- Two dice

Give it a try

1. Design a mazelike path from one side of the tiled or paved surface to the other. Lay out your path in string or draw it in chalk (ask permission if it's a tiled floor!).
2. Draw or take a photo of your maze on the ground so you can check it against how your "programmed" friend moves.
3. Write instructions to get from one end of the route to the other. It will go something like this:

   Move forward two squares;
   turn left;
   move forward three squares;
   turn through 90 degrees;
   move forward four squares.
4. Remove the chalk or string so your friend can't see the planned path.
5. Set your friend at the beginning of the route and start the stopwatch. Then read out the instructions, one at a time, for them to follow. Did they get to the correct finishing point? Stop the stopwatch when they reach the end.

Giving directions and calculating speed and *velocity* are important parts of the math of motion. This activity will give you the chance to "program" a friend to move along a route, then calculate their speed and velocity.

6. Using the tape measure, find the width of each tile or slab. Add up the number of tiles or slabs they have moved over and multiply by the size to find the total distance covered. Work out their speed from the time it took in feet or inches per second.

7. Can you work out their ***velocity?*** Measure from start to finish in a straight line and divide by how many seconds they took.

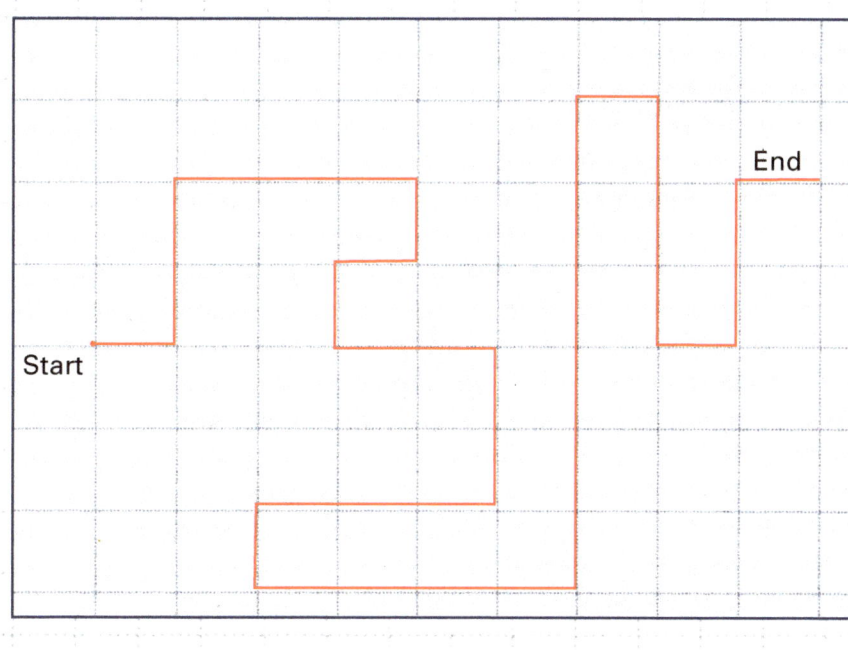

8. Now use dice to make up a random path. Throw one die to pick a direction: 1 is straight on, 2 is turn 90 degrees, 3 is turn 180 degrees, 4 is turn 270 degress. If you get a 5 or 6, throw again. Then throw the other die to see how many steps to take. Mark the route taken with chalk or string and time how long it takes to get from the starting point to the other side of the area. What was the speed?

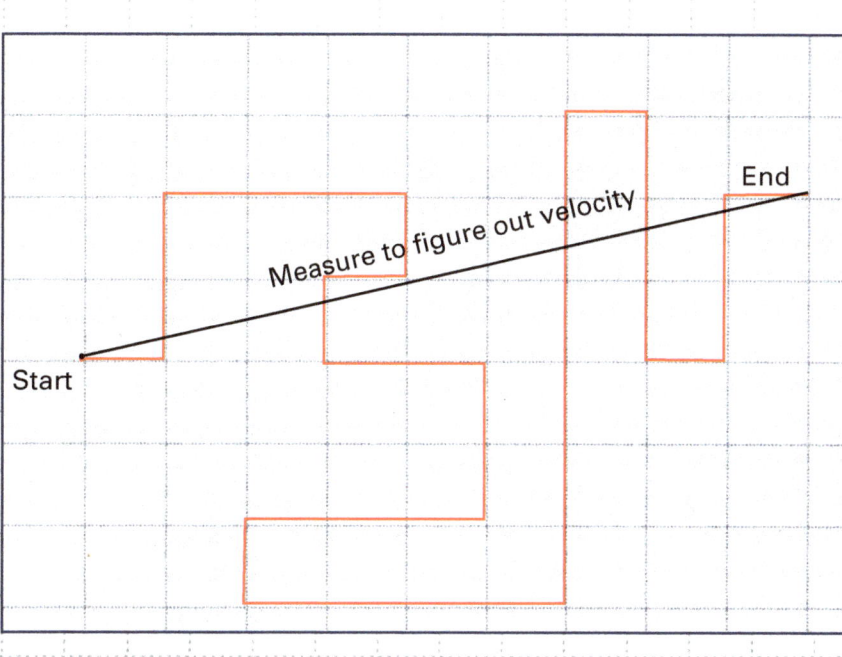

45

Index

A
absolute bearing, 13
acceleration, 19, 31, 39
air resistance, 34, 39
angles, 12-13, 23, 25, 28, 33, 37, 40-41
asteroids, 25

B
ballistics, 21
baseball, 23
bearing, 12-13
bicycling, 14-15
bowling, 22

C
car crashes, 24-25
centripetal force, 28

D
dandelion seeds, 38
degrees, 12-13, 28, 44-45
direction, 5, 8-14, 21, 23, 28, 31, 43-45
displacement, 18
drag, 34, 36

E
ellipses, 26-27
energy, 14, 19, 22-25, 40-41, 43
Europa Clipper (spacecraft), 31
evolution, 37

F
force, 5-6, 8, 14-15, 20-21, 23, 26, 28, 30, 40-41
friction, 34-35

G
Galilei, Galileo, 39
Global Positioning System (GPS), 11
gravity, 9, 28, 30-31, 33, 38, 40-41
gravity assist maneuvers, 31
Green, Anthony, 37

H
honey bees, 13
hypotenuses, 11

I
Ingenuity (helicopter), 33
inverse square law, 30

J
Johnson, Katherine, 9

K
Kepler, Johannes, 27
kites, 14

L
light, speed of, 17

M
Mars, 27, 31-33
molecules, 34, 42-43
momentum, 28, 40
moon, of Earth, 9, 23, 25, 28, 39, 41

N
Newton, Isaac, 21, 30
newtons, 20

O
orbits, 30-31

P
parabolas, 40-41
parachutes, 33, 35, 38
Perseverance (rover), 33
photons, 43
pool (game), 23

R
racing, 37
radiuses, 26, 28
relative bearing, 10, 12

resistance, 34, 39
right triangles, 11
rockets, 20-21, 33

S
satellites, artificial, 11, 30
Scott, David, 39
Shepard, Alan, 41
skateboarding, 9, 21
solar sails, 19
speed, 5, 8-9, 14, 16-19, 21, 23, 30, 32, 43, 45
spin art, 29
streamlining, 36-37, 39
sun, 17, 19, 27, 32, 43

T
tangents, 28-29
tennis, 20
trajectories, 40-41

V
vacuum, 34
vaporization, 23
velocity, 18-19, 23, 25, 31, 45

Z
Zander, Friedrich, 31

Glossary

absolute (AB suh loot)—can be measured from any starting point, with direction given in the same way from anywhere

acceleration (ak SEHL uh RAY shuhn)—increase (or decrease) in speed over time

air resistance (air rih ZIHS tuhns)—the effect of the air slowing down a moving object as its particles must be pushed aside

ballistics (buh LIHS tihks)—the study or science of how projectiles such as rockets and torpedoes move

bearing (BAIR ihng)—the horizontal angle between two objects or positions, or between one object or position and north

centripetal force (sehn TRIHP uh tuhl fohrs)—a force that makes a body follow a curved or circular path

displacement (dihs PLAYS muhnt)—shortest distance between a starting point and end point

drag (drag)—the slowing effect of moving through a fluid, such as air or water

ellipse (ih LIHPS)—oval

evolve (ih VOLV)—gradually change over time

force (fohrs)—a push or pull acting on an object

friction (FRIHK shuhn)—the force that acts between moving objects or a moving object and a surface, slowing the movement

gravity (GRAV uh tee)—the force that acts between objects that have mass, drawing them toward each other

molecule (MOL uh kyool)—tiny particle of matter, made up of atoms

momentum (moh MEHN tuhm)—a moving object's velocity, mulitpled by its mass

newton (unit) (NOO tuhn)—the force needed to make a mass of one kilogram (2.2 lb) accelerate at a rate of one metre (3.3 ft) per second squared

orbit (AWR biht)—to follow a curved path around an object, such as a planet or star

parabola (puh RAB uh luh)—symmetrical path that has a sloped line approaching and then going away from a curved peak or trough

photon (FOH ton)—tiny parcel of energy, often light energy

radius (RAY dee uhs)—the distance from the center of a circle to the edge

relative (REHL uh tihv)—depending on the starting position

resistance (rih ZIHS tuhns)—an opposing force

satellite (SAT uh lyt)—a natural or artificial object that goes around a planet or star

streamlined (STREEM LYND)—with a smooth shape that moves easily through a fluid such as water or air

tangent (TAN juhnt)—a line drawn from the edge of a circle forming a right angle with the radius (a line to the center of the circle)

trajectory (truh JEHK tuhr ee)—the path taken by a moving object

vacuum (VAK yum)—a space containing no matter, not even air or other gases

vaporize (VAY puh ryz)—to change state to become a gas

velocity (vuh LOS uh tee)—speed of an object moving in a specific direction

www.ingramcontent.com/pod-product-compliance
Lightning Source LLC
Chambersburg PA
CBHW061252170426
43191CB00041B/2415